No Time For Miracles

No Time For Miracles
Jack Veasey

YARDBIRD
Philadelphia & Bar Harbor

ISBN 0-9620251-1-9

ACKNOWLEDGEMENTS: Some of the poems in this book appeared previously in the following publications, *Oxalis, The Painted Bride Quarterly, The Irish Edition, Zone: A Feminist Journal for Women & Men, The Philadelphia Daily News, The South St. Star,* and *Manscape 2,* as well as in the chapbooks "The Truth of Blue" (Wit's End Press, Hershey, Pennsylvania, 1983) and "Tourist Season" (Slash & Burn Press, Philadelphia, Pennsylvania, 1984).

Cover drawing by Jeff King
This book is made from acid-free paper.

FIRST EDITION

Editorial Correspondence:
Yardbird Books
9 Strawberry Hill
Bar Harbor, Maine 04609

Library of Congress Cataloging-in-Publication Data

Veasey, Jack, 1955-
    No time for miracles / Jack Veasey. -- 1st ed.
        p. cm.
    ISBN 0-9620251-1-9 (alk. paper)
    I. Title.
    PS3572.E25N6   1989
    811'.54--dc20   89-39402
                                                              CIP

CONTENTS

"His weariness is that of the gladiator after the combat; his work was the whitewashing of a corner in a state official's office."

Franz Kafka

Blueprint

POOR MAN'S POETRY

Those who have everything
money can buy
often have nothing
money can't buy —
which may be why there's nothing
so rude as polite society,
no-one so cruel as those who claim
to have more class
than others. Though it may be crass,
I sing
in praise of those whose poverty
is outward only: those whose hands are empty
but whose hearts are full,
who feel love's pull,
who feel the lull
that peace provides, who feel no shame
in who they are. For them I wish what's priceless
if not perfect.
I suspect
they'll see the light behind
the flaw. Eyes bright with sadness
are not blind.

EPISTLE FOR THE TWO THIEVES

They did not have immaculate mothers,
nor fathers with patience sufficient
to be cuckolded by God
and keep on smiling,
keep on working at a trade.
They did not have disciples, nor bright visions
anybody might write down.

They did not have the network of advantages
that put Him
in the center
of the picture:
the homeless
have no time for miracles.

I want to read a Bible
about them:
a Bible that asks *why*
the wrong go wrong —
we all *know* HOW —
a Bible where the price
is here and now,
that holds out hope of Heaven
when we've made the payments.

A Bible for those too poor
to be meek, that we too
may inherit
something;
a Bible for the people
who start bleeding many years before
the nails are driven in
officially;

10

a Bible for the people
born in Hell,
like some of us,

and like our fathers.

Foundations

GOING TO FIRES

Because we were too poor
to go to movies or museums,
and because there often were
no corner brawls or pick-up playground baseball games,
the sirens would call me like voices sometimes,
and I'd follow

but first I'd go and find my father
deep in Kelly's bar,
dodging darts as I did so
and slipping on sawdust
and cringing at shuffleboard clacks,
ducking under drunks' arms

I was maybe five years old
and horrified by gawking at the gutter, brass,
beneath the bar's black bottom,
beneath the feet of men who sat on stools
and spat and hurled their snot there too, cigar butts,
anything exhaled

and I was more horrified still
by the sight of old Kelly —
a double amputee from diabetes
always scooting back and forth behind the bar,
waiting on people from his wheelchair,
while his mangy midget dog
snarled in his lap

and always it was Dad who found me first,
for I'd have gotten lost in looking at these things

and there would be no need to say a word,
for he'd have heard the sirens, too

and he would scoop me up and carry me
to where, by now, the crowd had always gathered,
some in slippers, some in curlers,
all of them guessing about
which bad kid had set *this* one,
and gossiping about the little loss
for this week's victims (the church
would take care of them, surely, and who owned
one thing of value anyway?)

and gaping at the maze of hoses
strewn across the street,
and at the flames beyond smashed windows
and the smoke that reached the sky, freer
than we were

and enjoying this, the evening's entertainment,
this brief breather from our boredom,
and wondering — though never worrying —
about whose house would go
next week, in sacrifice
to certain
urban
gods.

This was before
there were many good
murders
to watch.

CHILDREN AT PLAY

I stand
on the roof,
with three stories beneath me
abandoned, a few rooms
burned out, and much more than a few
filthy windows
long broken by bricks.
I move
to the edge
of the roof, looking down
at my risk:

an alley piled
with rotting garbage,
broken glass, boards
armed with nails, sharp smells, snarls
of shed clothing even bums
would never touch.
I see one brave rat
scurry by, though I know
there are more.

This is where I'll fall
if I should fall.

I stand on the edge of the roof,
and I make up my mind.
I breathe and feel
more deeply than I think.
I have not learned to say no,
but neither have I learned
to not fear to say yes.
And I am old enough
to never be afraid,
according to the other boys.
I am, after all,
eleven.

It isn't the fall that I fear most,
I know: it's the sneering and jeering
right here, maybe fists too
to follow.

I stand
on the edge, swallow
sickly, and
make up my mind.

I back
up, gulp
dank air for good luck,
and run
to the edge.

I jump off
as hard
as I
know how.

I jump
from the edge
into air, into
danger; I jump
into the moment
of not knowing.

For that moment
I am free, the ones who dared me
distant
as dead dreams, though
for that moment
there is neither
death
nor broken bones for me, nor
bruising, burning
accusations.
There is only
terrified
exhilaration, something
like a glimpse
of God.

Then I crash
to the roof
of the next house,
feet first;
losing balance,
I fall
on my face, scrape
my knees, come up
filthy. I pick myself up
from the roof, feeling
shocked
but undamaged.

From across the alley
I can hear
applause,
but it's a bitter victory.

I have only been forgiven
till the next time.

PLAYGROUND SCAPEGOAT

Remember him? The one
you persecuted, mocked, humiliated,
punched, pelted with rocks?
The one with the pained eyes
behind thick glasses, puny, face
seething with acne?
That one:
while you drew blood, well,
he drew
pictures.

It was you
who gave to him
the gift of
rage —
rage that the bland or normal
never once imagine.
Rage
that builds cities, spews novels,
sings high notes, makes
myth
of a whole life's mistakes.
Rage that risks everything
till what was dreamt
turns real...
the rage of the driven
to win.

It is his book
you hold in your hands;
his memory
from which you run
forever, never
going
anywhere.

Neighbors

WILLIE

He's a 35-year-old grocery boy —
"a little slow," or so
some people say.
He doesn't envy them
their speed.

He sweeps the church out weekly, too,
and grins
despite the priests
who patronize him.
He grins because he knows
some secret things.

He knows, for instance, that his mother
is a goddess, though most people think
she's just the crossing guard.
He knows, too, that she loves him most
of all her children, since he has the gift
to listen.

He knows
what silence says in church
on Saturday. And he knows all the secrets
of the stained glass angels, who wear grins
not unlike his.

Best of all, he knows
that there is time to think
when no-one makes demands,
or tries to ask you anything.

He'll never have to be
"a good provider."

MARIE

These days, she seldom ventures
from the row-house, except to shop
or take food to a neighbor.
She cooks for the ones
who are sick in their sixties, not healthy
the way she stayed somehow.
What she gets in return is the feeling
there's someone to cook *for*; that's a lot,
if cooking was your job for years.

Otherwise, for company, she has three dogs —
more constant than grown children —
and the small army of strays
that haunt her doorstep.
Father Cahill, she heard someone say,
once nicknamed her
"the patron saint of strays."

The only saint she'll worship still
is Charlie. She has photos of him
on her every wall, surrounding her,
keeping her safe. Somehow
these are more real to her
than anything that happens on the street.
Her favorite is the one above the bed:
he's back on the deck of the old boat,
shirt off, sweating, wrestling
with an angry rope,
and swearing.
He's not a young man anymore,
but he was *never*
more the man she married.

Those were his last years, the longest;
his fishing was by then only a hobby,
though he still stuck
to deep-sea.
On weekdays he and she worked
in the luncheonette they'd bought, which bore
her name. She remembers the voices
of truckers, the comforting catcalls,
the way they ribbed him
and he razzed them back. He, like her,
was everybody's friend. He'd fix up their broken machines
while she cooked up their meals.
He taught her, never saying so,
that what you do
determines what you are. She, too,
never put it into words,
but it's a lesson she still lives —
hers is still the house all neighbors often visit.

But her loneliness
is for one person only,
one whose heart gave out, no warning,
one hot weekend out at sea.
That taught her you can die
of loving something.

So she plays
the plastic Emenee chord organ
that he gave her as a joke, plays
by the numbers, plays
the ones they used to dance to…

knowing that a boat will come
to take her
too.

DONNY

Donny drank, you know,
for years and years.
Some people even saw him sleeping
in the gutter;
shades were drawn
when he came
knocking,
pounding,
shouting.
But since his brother had that stroke
he sobered up.

Now he comes down each day,
to take Pinkie
for walks in the wheelchair
and help out with housework.
No matter what he does, though,
Pinkie's wife still hates him;
treats him like a little kid,
talks down to him
like he was dirt, or less
than dirt.
The neighbors
can see it,
but nobody
says anything.

He lives in a rooming house,
no phone, and five stops away.
When Pinkie goes
God knows how soon
he'll know it.
Still can't find a job, to boot;
and being 53, a man gets
fewer chances.

Sometimes you say hello,
and you can see he wonders
what he can't remember,
what might be some reasons
why. You want to tell him
it was luck, that's all — the bottle struck
like Pinkie's stroke. You want
to forgive him, as if it was you
who got hurt. But you can't remember yourself
what exactly was missing,
what didn't make sense.

And when he forgets to shave
you worry, wonder
if what happened isn't
over

though the wheelchair
keeps on creaking
down the street,

and though some people say
that Donny
is a saint,

now that it's these days
and
not
those

ZEKE

He stands in the cold
in a space suit
made out of asbestos...but no,
he's not
on the moon. That'd be
an event.

No, this day's only one
in a blur of identical days —
maybe Wednesday
or Thursday.
He's standing
in the freezer room
of some unseen man's
ice cream factory.

He feels as though he's been here
all his life — although he knows
it's not a year yet — since today
it's been ten hours.
They tell him it'll be fifteen
before he's through.
It's mandatory overtime here,
every day
of his six-day work week, though
unofficially, of
course.

What he does is stand here,
at the end of this
ten-foot conveyor belt.
The canisters of ice cream,
thirty pounds apiece, pop through
the little doors, and ride along the belt
to meet him. They come in spurts
of five or six at once.
He has to snatch them off the belt
and stack them
on a palette, fast;
if one should fall, they say
it's him who'll pay.
The second any bunch is done,
another's on its way.

At first it made him nervous;
now it's boring, deadly boring,
though it doesn't leave him time
to fantasize, or make up word games
in his head; too fast — takes all
his concentration.

It's lucky the pain
in his lower back
keeps him awake, though he's told
he'll get used to that.
It feels normal
to the guys who've been here
ten years, or thirteen; that's
most of the guys,
so they tell him.
They say he'll forget it
the way he forgets about
dreams.
Still, afterwards, he'll go home
and collapse, too tired
to even watch TV.

Then on Sunday, at the bar,
he'll spend his money...
until he's drunk enough
to wait for Monday.

One day, he hopes,
he'll spend his Sundays
with a wife, though he has no idea
how or when
he'll find one.

First, he'll have to find
the time.

THE DOCTOR

He tells you that your health
will have to wait
till after lunch,
till after golf,
till 9 AM two weeks from Monday.

He tells you any question he can't answer
is a question not worth asking.

He tells you
you need a vacation
that nobody but a doctor
could afford.

He tells you to strip
and you do, just like a whore
except that *you*
are paying for it.

You make fists,
breathe deeply, you wait
till your heartbeats are counted.
You do all that he tells you
on command.

You cough
with your balls in his hand.

MICKIE

He pays in quarters
for his bottle of
Wild Irish Rose,
and he laughs out loud
right in the liquor store.

He's haunted by the ghosts of
teeth
the way some are by those
of limbs
or lovers —
which is lucky or unlucky
by comparison, depending
on your viewpoint.

This time of year,
with all the stuffy noses,
fewer people
pull away, though
there are always those
who do.

But his buddies
always give him big hellos
as he holds court
out on the corner, collecting
for the deep red god
each day, no matter
what the weather is.

And when he sleeps, enveloped
in the warmth of vents
that steam beneath him
lovingly, he dreams
like anybody.
Sometimes he dreams
about how fat he used to be; he's happy
he's not that way now.

Five years ago,
before The Fall,
there was a family
that called him
"Father"

THE COMFORTER

He lives out of a locker
at the Greyhound station.
He gets by the guard
with a ticket he found
months ago; the guard
just thinks he travels a lot.

For the guard's sake, somehow,
he stays always
clean. This sometimes hurts him
when he begs for money
for his one meal at McDonald's,
and admission to the movie
where he sleeps. He doesn't mind
that those who pay his wages
seem convinced he isn't sane —
he feels safer
now that no-one knows his name,
and what he did
before
grows daily dimmer.
He feels proud, instead, of what
he doesn't do:
steal, drink, or sell
his blood or body.

And besides,
he isn't *really*
out of work.
His job
is to make men
generous
again.

VIDEO WHIZ

Beneath his reflection
and through his reflection
small creatures with snapping jaws
flee, chased across
the glass minefield

He steers not with his hands
but his whole body: twists
his hips, lifts
one sneak off the floor, knees
bending, yanks
the short black stick,
and something living
swerves
into oblivion

He smirks when the electric voices
chirp their hectic, repetitious
hornpipe; explosions
only serve to coax him
deeper

He has learned to play the pandemonium —
to turn the tables
on the creatures that pursue him
through the maze of his new mind...
a mind unblemished
by the dusty books
that didn't teach
about the street,
that dazed him

Here, everything
is razor-
sharp, all reflexes at ready
as in sex, as in a car chase on TV

Here he is
Black, Hispanic, Asian, or Caucasian,
anything
and many things

His is now
the kind of world
where any kid
can win

ON GETTING A LIFT

Really, he sings
to all his passengers,
and so far nobody
has shot him.

He doesn't look much like the type
to serenade you —
unshaven, middle-aged, built
like a bricklayer, his shoulders
bulging through
the sleeveless t-shirt he wears
even in the winter,
with the cab's heat cranked up high.
Red foam rubber dice
hang from his rear-view mirror.

Anyway, he starts to play
a tape of Luther Vandross,
really loud; then asks
if the rider likes the voice; then says
that Vandross is his idol.
In fact, he says, he sings
himself — and with a band,
about to cut a record.

By now, Vandross
has eased into "Superstar,"
a sad love song
by Leon Russell, and he starts
to sing along.
And, amazingly, he sounds
a lot like Vandross — sometimes
powerful, sometimes
ethereal, a gospel voice
that somersaults
and dips and soars,
dreamily steaming up the windshield.
Pretty good,
up to a point; the guy's got
soul, and almost
perfect pitch.

You know the line about the record
is a lie, of course,
when he forgets the words,
too lost in sound
to cling to meaning.

But by now
you're almost
home, and no-one
thinks about their troubles
in *this* cab,

and yes, you'll tip
accordingly.

THE SUN MAKES ITS ROUNDS

What is it about him, exactly —
his laugh, the way it seems to be derisive,
but is followed by a wink?
His walk, which would seem cocky
if it weren't so relaxed?
The way he flirts with the whole world
so openly?

Though he pushes a trash-can on wheels
through a building where men in suits rule,
he is King of the Roost.
Most of the women want him,
though few would admit it; they prefer
to flirt with strength, but sleep
with power. No matter:

he knows what he's learned
from those moments
when time was his own,
when he walked into water
and cast his hook into the depths.

He defies the bosses
with a grin, and they respect his limits,
though they don't know why.

He shows peers the ropes with a joke
that lasts longer than lessons
in your cluttered memory.
He knows what truth you sense in him, though
you will never call him
as you see him:
hero, father, brother, friend.
He only works here —
that's his deal with them, and you.

He knows that time-cards are no more
than paper; hours mean little
to a man years don't diminish.
What he has to do
does not define him:

he chooses his way.
He has not been tamed.

Walls and Windows

NO SHOES, NO SHIRT, NO SERVICE

no shoes
no shirt
no service.
no smoking
no parking
no four-letter words on the air.
no contest.
no cause for alarm.

no unsolicited manuscripts.
no unescorted ladies.
no minors unaccompanied by adult.

no pets in this building.
no visitors after eleven.
no fraternizing with the customers.
no fraternizing with the staff.
no fraternizing with the students and
no contest, no way.
no cause for alarm.

no place like home.
no time like the present.
no fool like an old fool.
no such thing as Santa Claus.

no dice.
no wonder.
no booze till your urine's normal.
no sex till the big game's over.
no erections till you're out of boot camp.
no way.
no more Mr. Nice Guy.

no gravity on the moon.
no gravy on the mashed potatoes.
no bloodshed on television.
no films that the Church condemns.
no meat on Friday either, and
no contest, no dice.
no cause for alarm.

no public nudity beyond this point.
no ghetto blasters without headphones.
no conversation in the library.
no jacket,
no tie,
no admission.

no trespassing either.
no swimming.
no skating.
no dreams with this new medication.
no telling what's next.

GREY IMPRESSIONS

The ears believe other people;
the eyes believe themselves.

                -found in fortune cookie

The sound of no-one answering
the telephone next door; then,
distant sirens

***

Through the peeling wall I hear
their nightly war. I never see their faces,
but I know their names

***

No theory
so thin
as these walls

***

Half asleep, I hear tires
whoosh on rain-swept streets;
I ride the sound, unsettled

***

Always the sound of alarms.
Every weekday, waking's
an emergency

***

Brakes shriek, horns bleat, curses
fill the air
like scattered dandelion strands

***

Truant children under hydrants
squeal, delighted;
no firemen sleep this morning

***

It occurs to the daydreaming
office drone — that sound
might be typing, or rain

***

Here, where the neighbors
never say hello, the city still
is never silent

***

From his air-conditioned car,
the preacher sees the house
where windows break like spirits

***

In the pulsing sun, sweat
soaks the open shirt; tattoos
gleam, skin browns, buildings begin

***

The pamphlets promise peace
and happiness, but those who hand them out
look crazy

***

In uniform, he holds the door
for pampered people, smug but unsuspecting;
remembering, preferring this to prison

***

Stray dog sniffs
a toppled garbage can,
delicious

***

Stairwell or hotel?
They shuffle amid urine fumes,
wearing fine masks of grime

***

A nearly naked man lies drowsing
on a steaming vent, by drafts
undaunted

***

She leans on the traffic light,
strapped into satin; she smiles
as the bidding begins

***

Bars, on the windows even
of the very rich; sleep,
and the ghosts of broken glass

***

She sorts damp clothing
in the all-night laundromat; again,
an odd number of socks

***

Across the street from church
all night, new neon
winking

***

A cockroach crawls,
half-looped, around the rim
of an abandoned can of beer

***

The man on the TV screen,
black and white,
watching us sleep

SUDDENLY SPRING IN SOUTH PHILLY

Sirens, jackhammers, and 4 AM quarrels next door
don't wake me anymore. But today, outside my window,
I heard *birds.* My eyes opened and the plastic
on the window wasn't stirring, and the light
that filtered in was gold, not grey.
In one layer of clothes I ran down the stairs,
out the door, onto the street
where the doors of the stores stood wide open.
People sauntered by in shirtsleeves
and unhurried, sighing in relief, as though aware
a truce had been declared.

LINES ON MY MOTHER'S HANDS

No matter where
I find myself, I find I'm
very much
my mother's son...

my mother who, at
sixty plus, still
picks up after strangers
for a living,
she

who rummages in
wastebaskets from which
to pluck
gems
for the memory

What other people throw away
without a second look, what
those with too much money
won't consider, what
was lost but never
missed, what
was invisible
to eyes that wouldn't
see

my mother
finds, my mother
gathers:

she saves
relics of the saints
some people never
were nor even
dreamed
of being...

a grey, opaque bottle in which
rich wine's spirit
still lives;
an unread magazine where
last week's news still waits
for children it will matter to;
a thirsty plant, discarded
like a dead thing;
wide wall calendars across which
horses gallop, mountains
rise, white
rapids
foam;

postcards from
strange places that
might change the visitor
who sees the meaning, scrawled
with mundane messages, love
on the run, signed and
sent home from
places where they
wished
you
were

Many things
pass through
my mother's
hands, my mother's
hands

which crack from
years of
work, which make
these too-used rooms
come
clean,
which open
wide, alive,
reaching and
reaching

I see those hands
in mine, which write
of her, assembling
words
found in
the world

mending what was
broken
when the moment
hurried by,
recycling
what might otherwise be
lost

still passing something
fragile
on
and on

DEAR NEIGHBORS, ABOUT THAT NOISE...
(In memory of my grandmother)

Grandmom sang,
and that's not all that I remember, though
I often wish it were.
Grandmom sang,
and all the while
she cleaned
and cleaned
and cleaned, but it was the song
that swept away the cobwebs.

Grandmom sang,
despite the husband
who kept cursing her for years,
who cursed her even
after they removed his larynx —
his dirty words grown more obscene
though blurred by gruesome gurgling.

Grandmom sang,
despite the factory
that filled our lives with so much smoke
you couldn't see across the street
at noon, when the ear-splitting whistle blew.
Grandmom sang, and she kept singing
after two of her three children
simply walked off and forgot her
till the time came to come back
and split the spoils.

Only my mother
always understood the song.
"People who can sing should live forever,"
Mom said one day, and it's true
that Grandmom did outlive her husband —
though senility
made her forget her songs.
And when *she* died the crumbling church
was filled for the first time in, well,
God knows.

Nobody sang at that service
except in our heads.

No, people who can sing
don't live forever,
but the songs they sing continue.
I sing those songs still, songs
older than I am:

while I breathe the country air,
while I live with a lover
I need never marry,
while I pet the cat I got
instead of children,
while my dust collection grows.

Across the street I see
a cemetery,
and I see it very clearly
all day long, especially
when noon arrives.

You might say
it's noon
in my life,
now that I've slipped past thirty.

56

So I tell myself
I won't forget the songs,
and I sing out —
at times too loud,
at times too long.
Some neighbors say
it seems I'll sing
forever, and not
as a compliment.

But I think my dumbstruck neighbors
miss the point.
What tears at me
flies off, like birds
through smoke, in search
of some kind of clear sky.

And as for these assertions of forever, only I
am truly fooled —
and I suppose that could be why
I
keep
on
singing.

What Comes Knocking

Hands
that have worked
too hard, too long,
to ever be
completely
clean; hard
hands,
blunt-nailed,
beginning their descent
with unexpected
tenderness...

Hands
that have driven
nails
and cars
and danced
with basketballs
and sweating
breasts;
hands
that have been
somewhat
scarred
by what they've held, strong
hands
belonging to strong
arms...

Hands
that have maybe never
coaxed a statue
out of stone, beats
from a drum, breath
from a newborn baby by
whacking its bum, but
hands
that surely have such powers,
among others...
Hands
you can't imagine
clasped in prayer.
Hands
by which there is no doubt
your hand was
shaken, dark hands,
hands
no glove has covered;
hands
without rings,
without watches,
mysterious,
free...

Bare
hands. Rough
hands.
Fit to cuff
your
face...

and yet,
instead,
they stroke
your
spine,
un-
wind-
ing
you
like something
furred
and purring...

Only hands like these
could strip you
of your sorrows.
Only hands like these
could bring you
to your knees.